NATURE DRAWING

AND

DESIGN

BY

FRANK ⁂ STEELEY

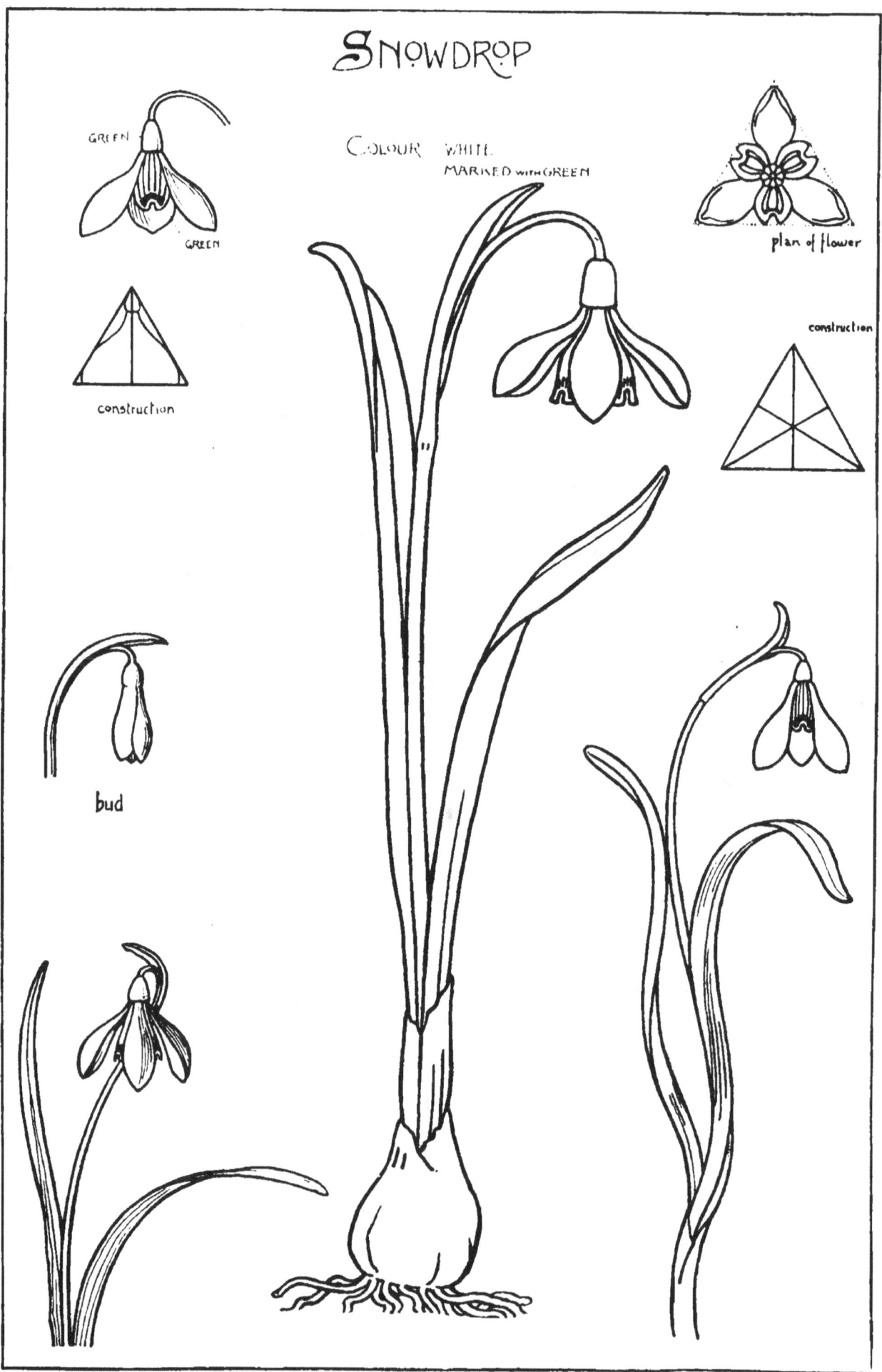

Plate II.

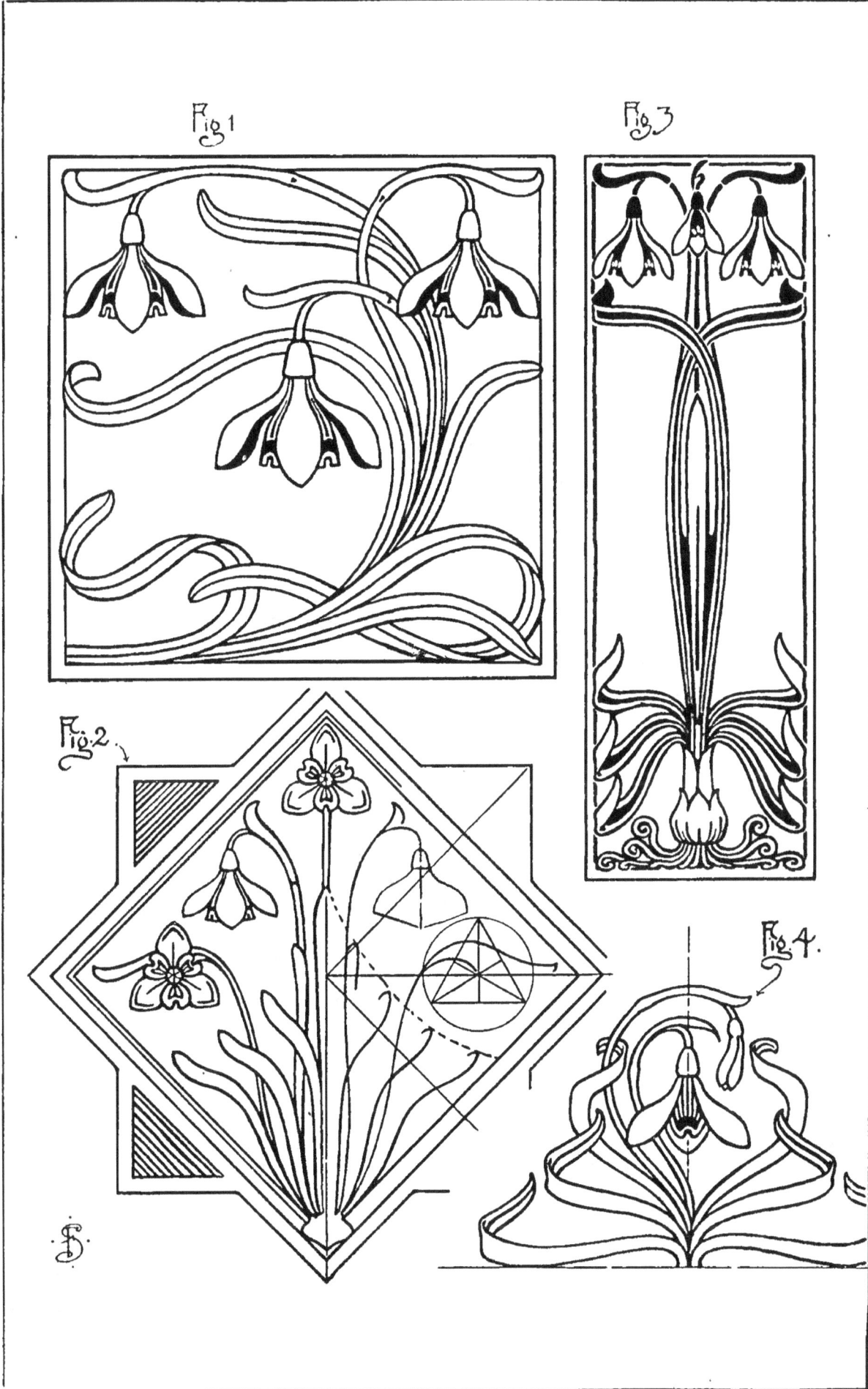

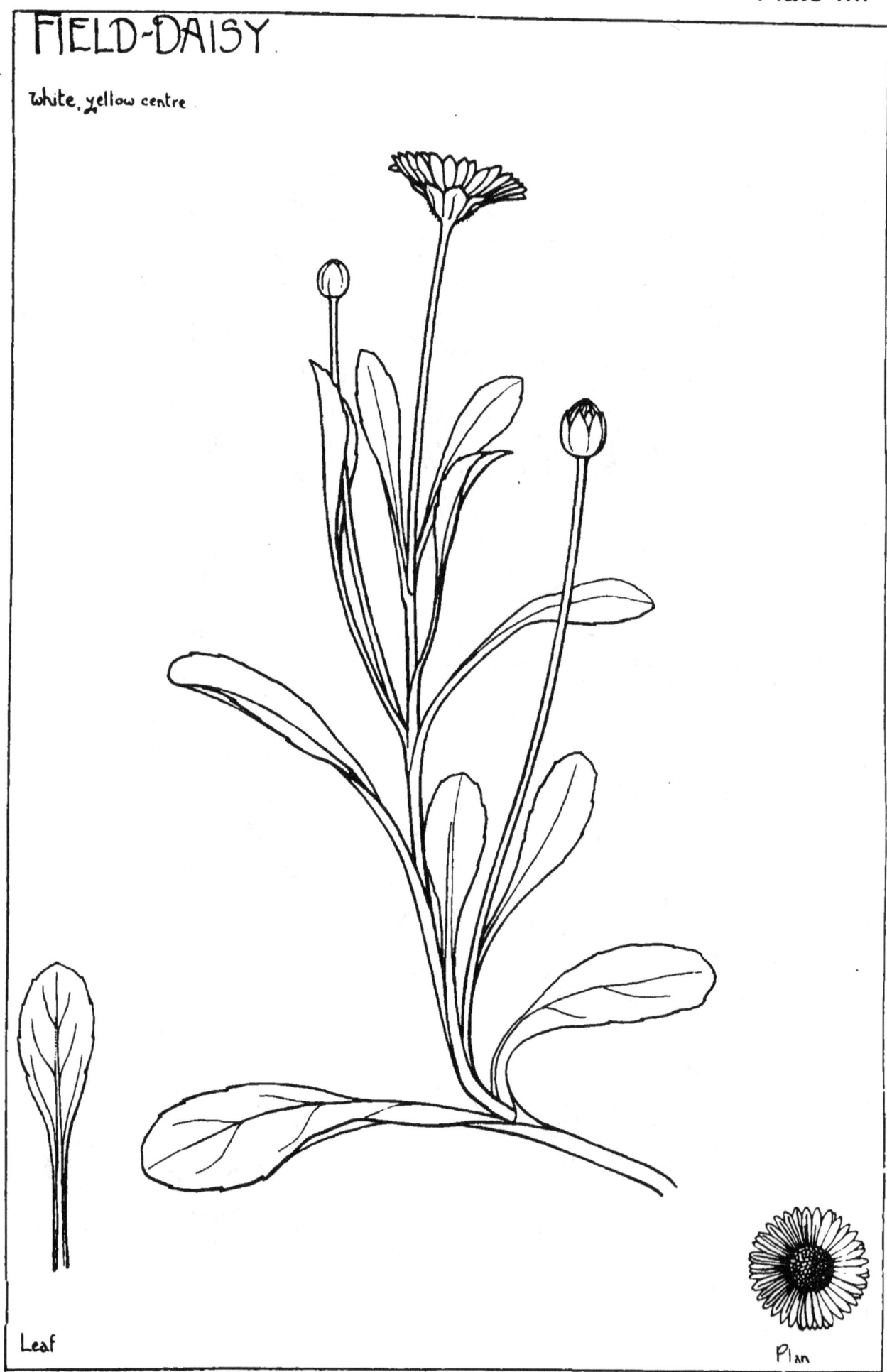

Plate IV.

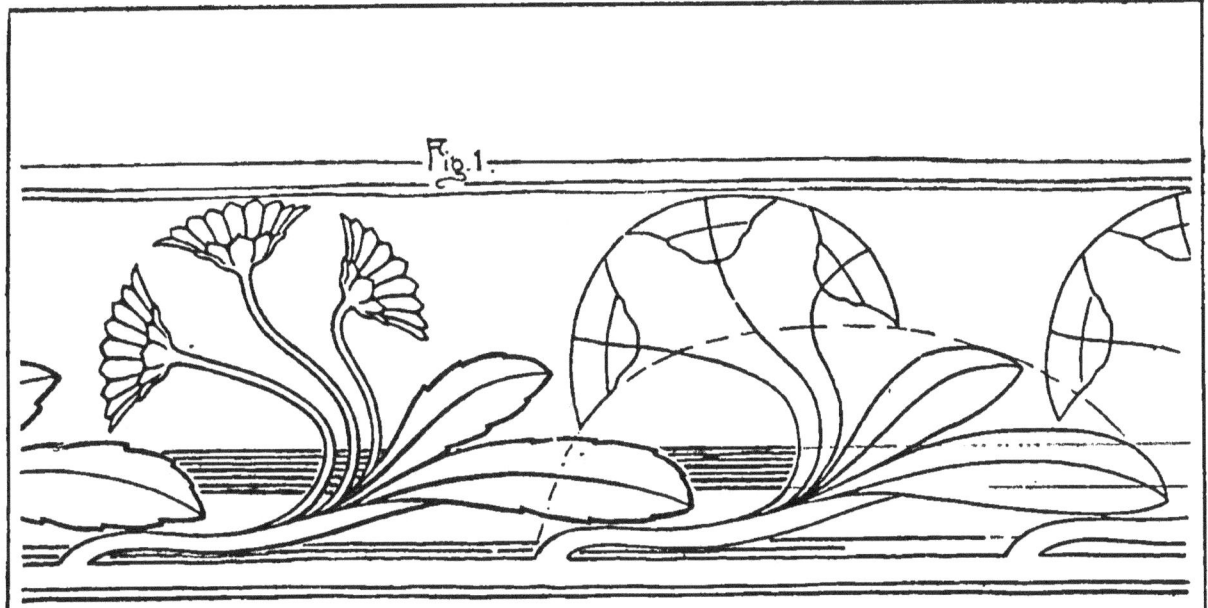

Fig. 1

REPEATING BORDER.

Fig. 2.

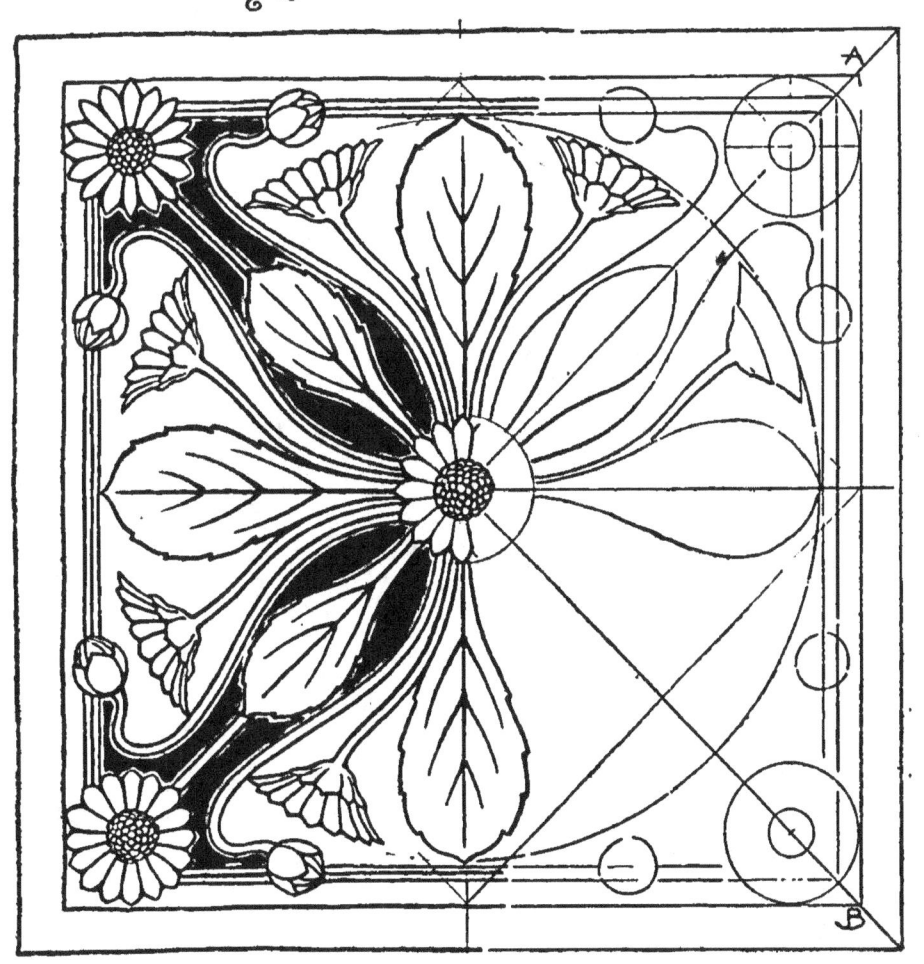

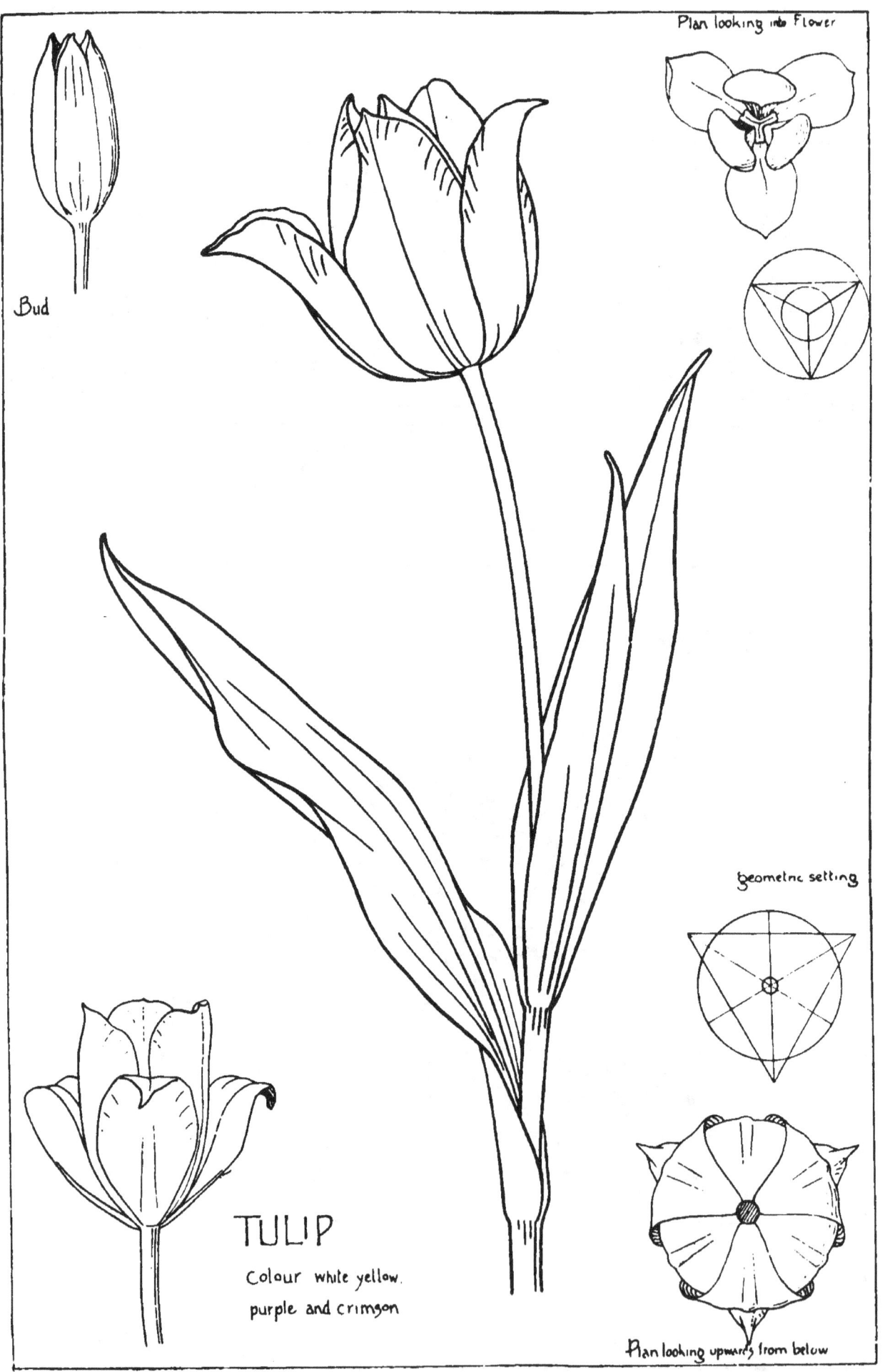

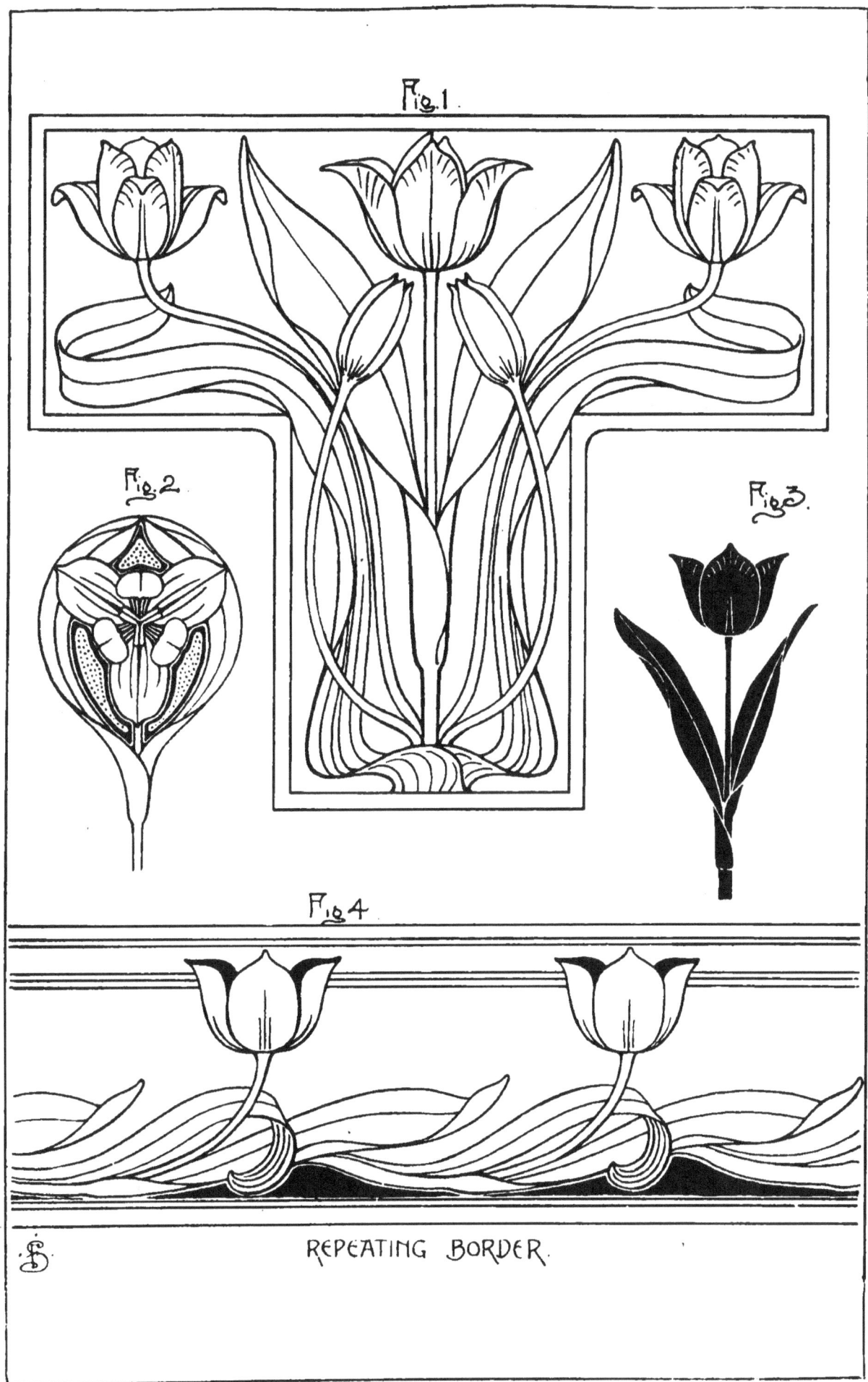

Plate VI.

REPEATING BORDER.

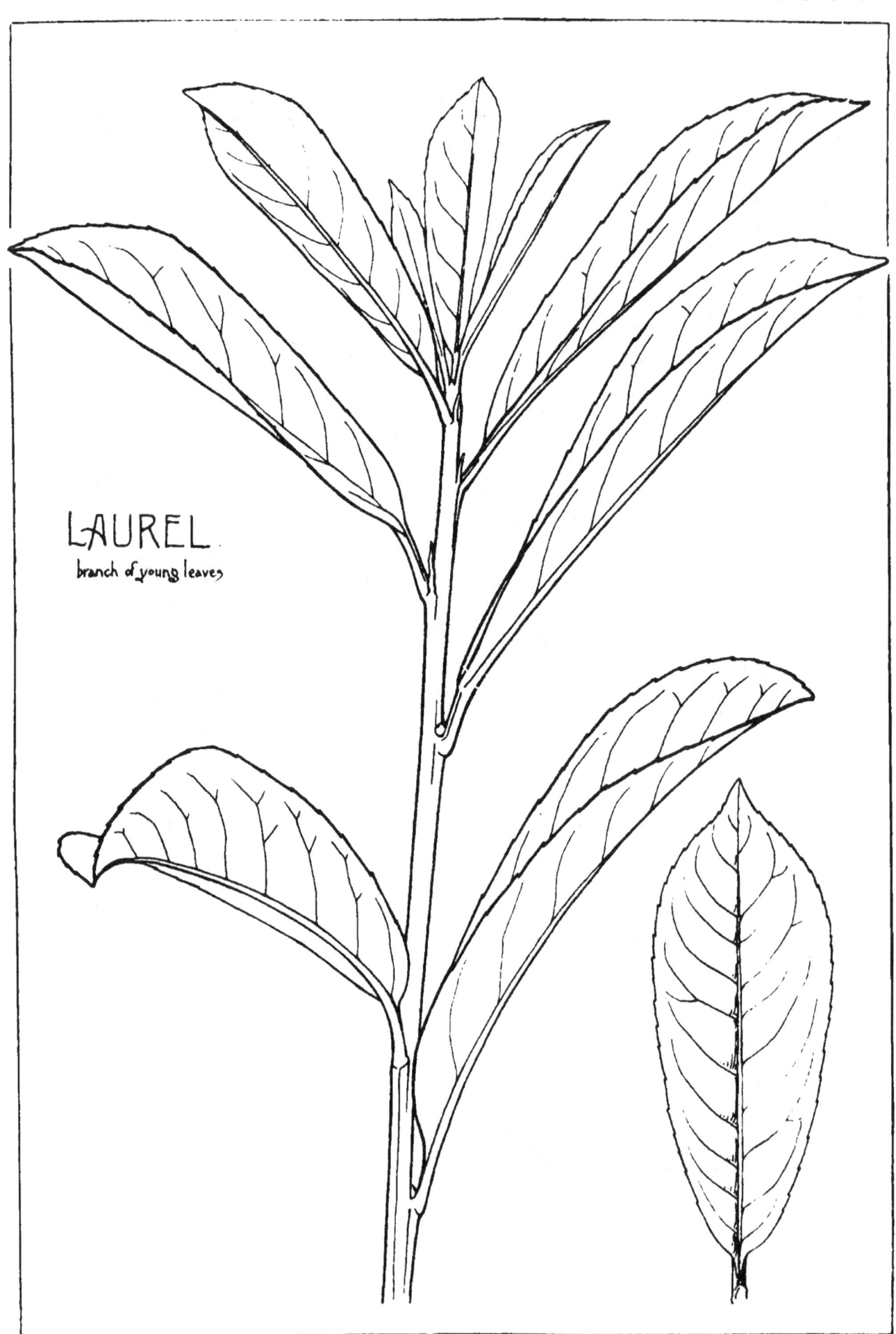

Plate VII.

LAUREL.
branch of young leaves

Plate VIII.

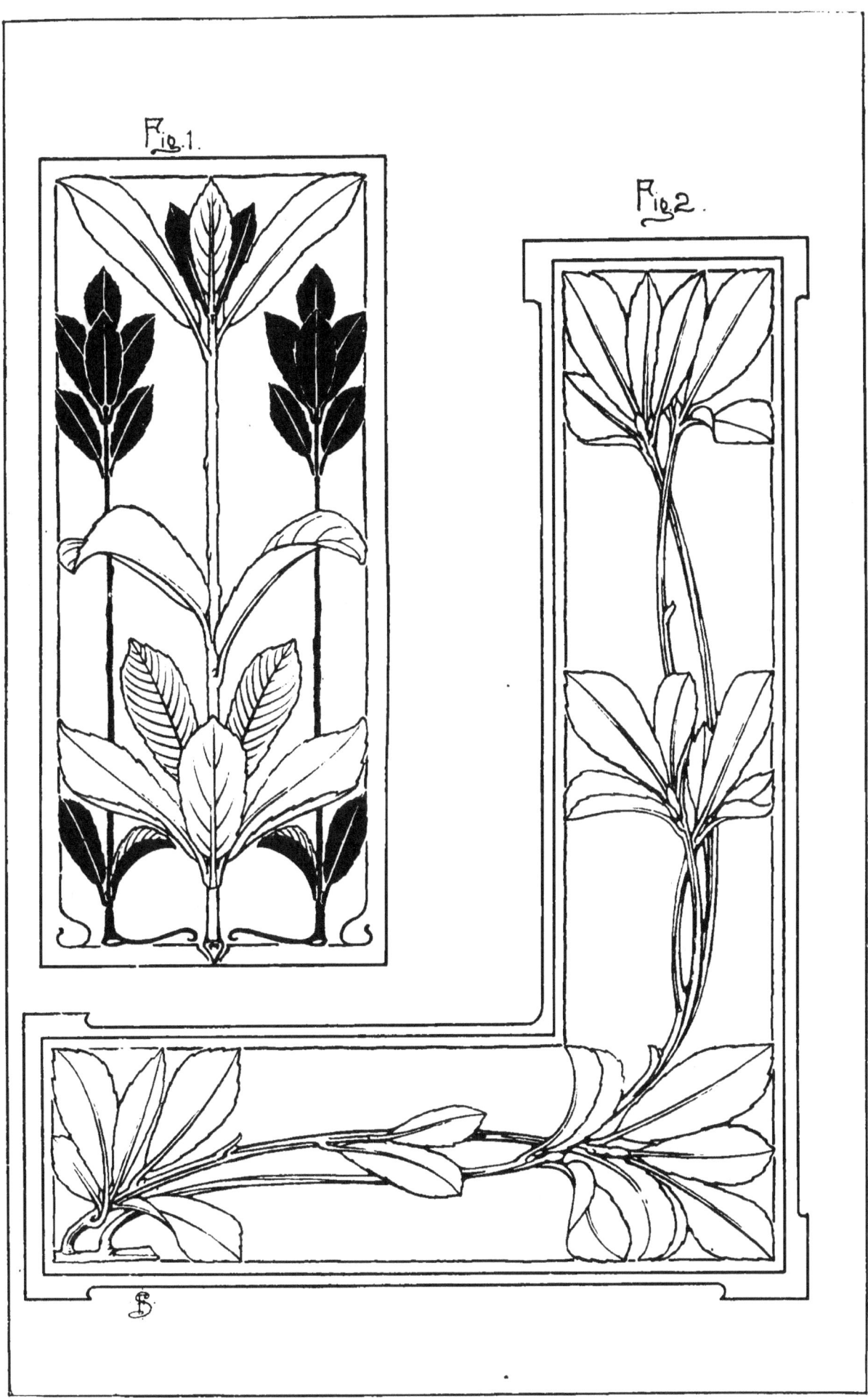

Fig. 1.

Fig. 2.

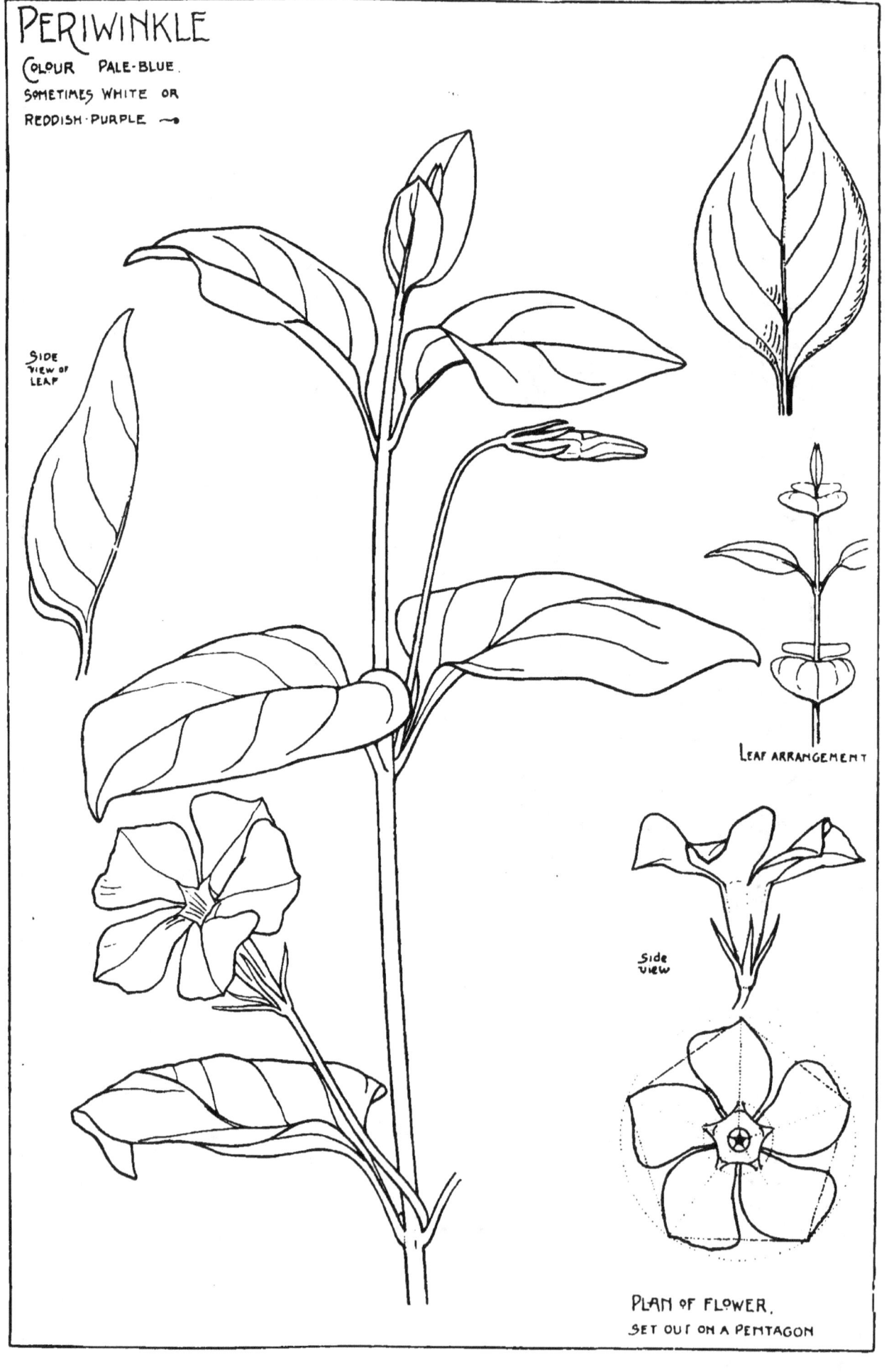

Plate X.

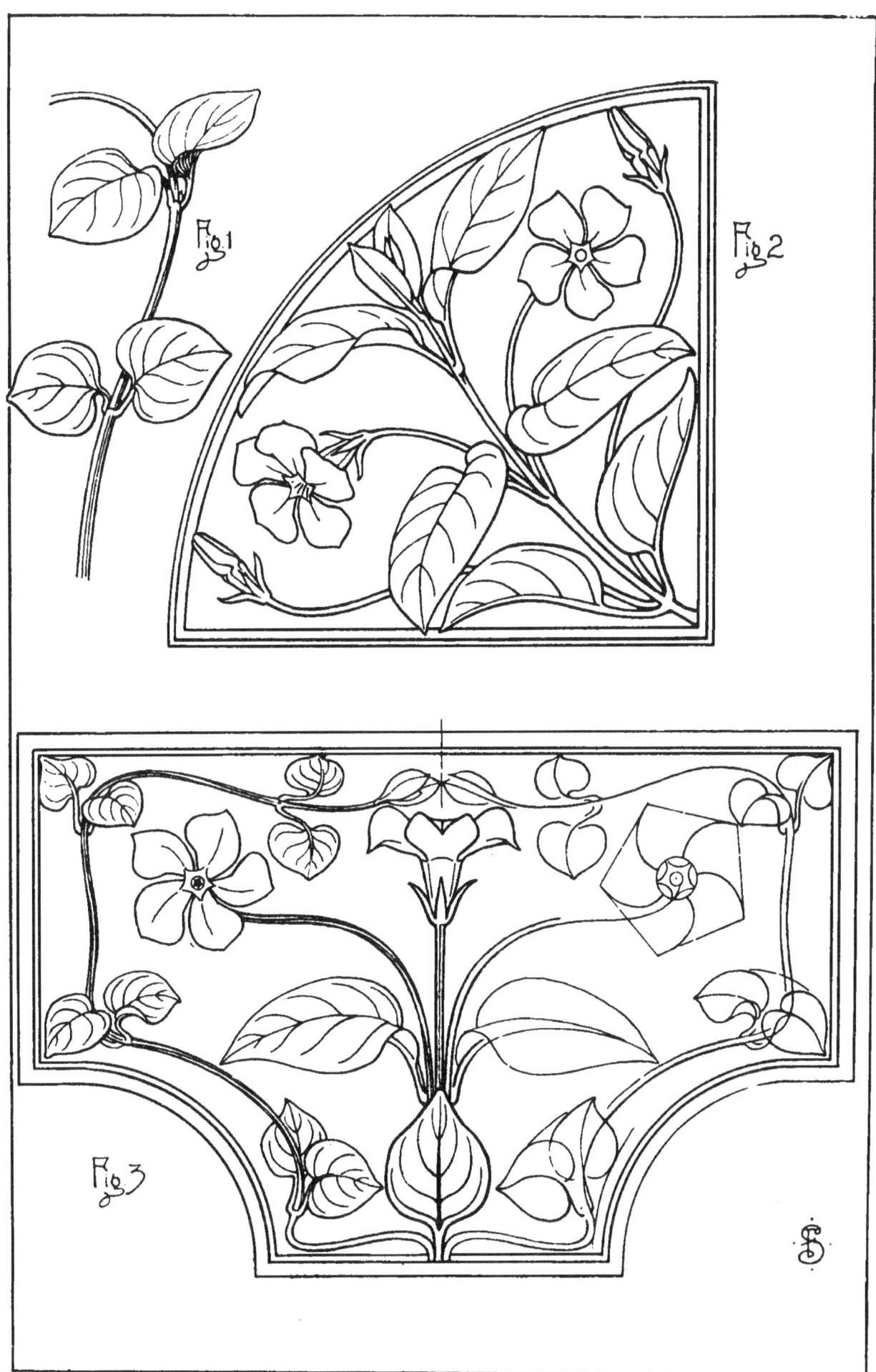

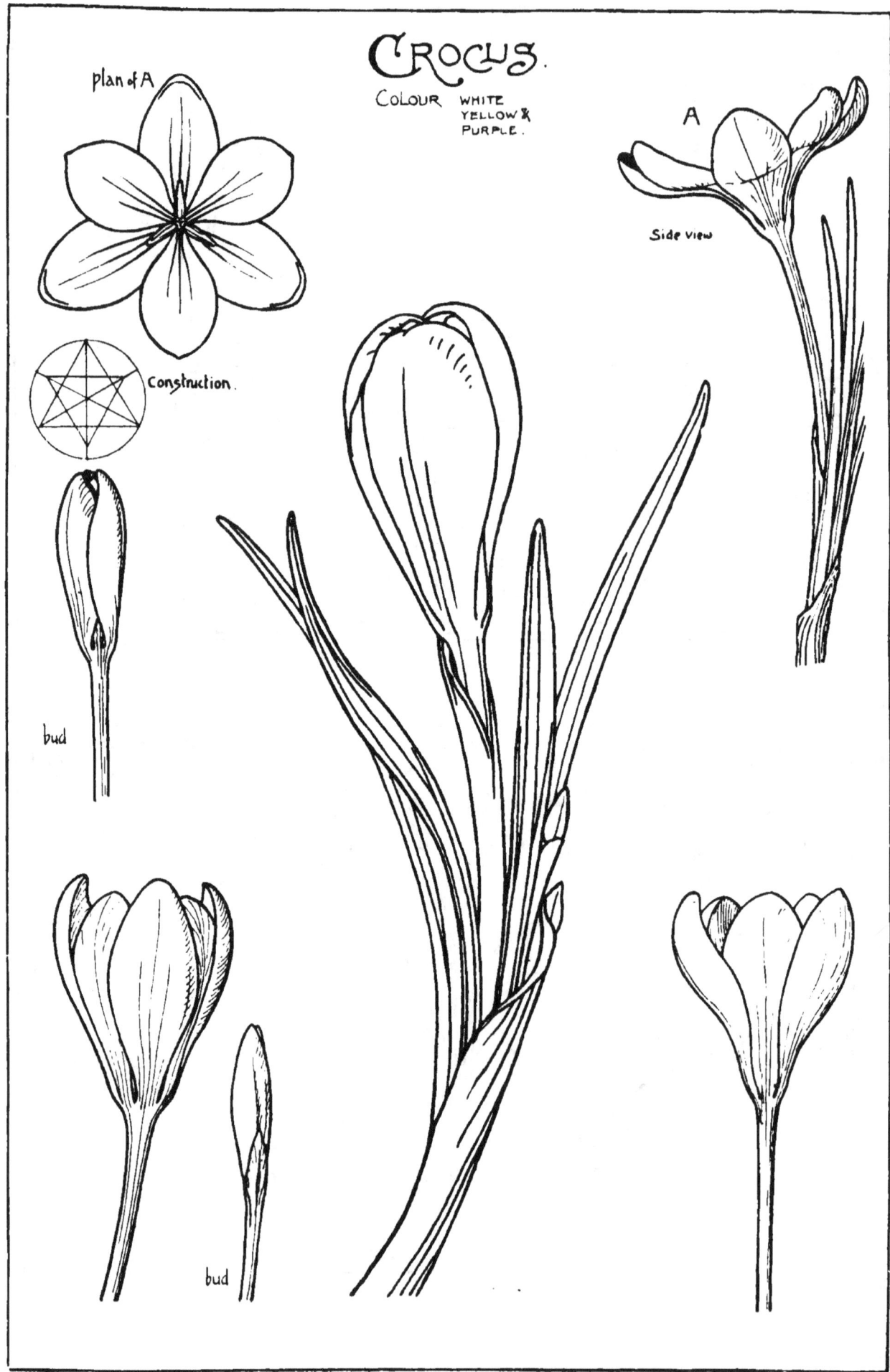

Plate XI.

Plate XII.

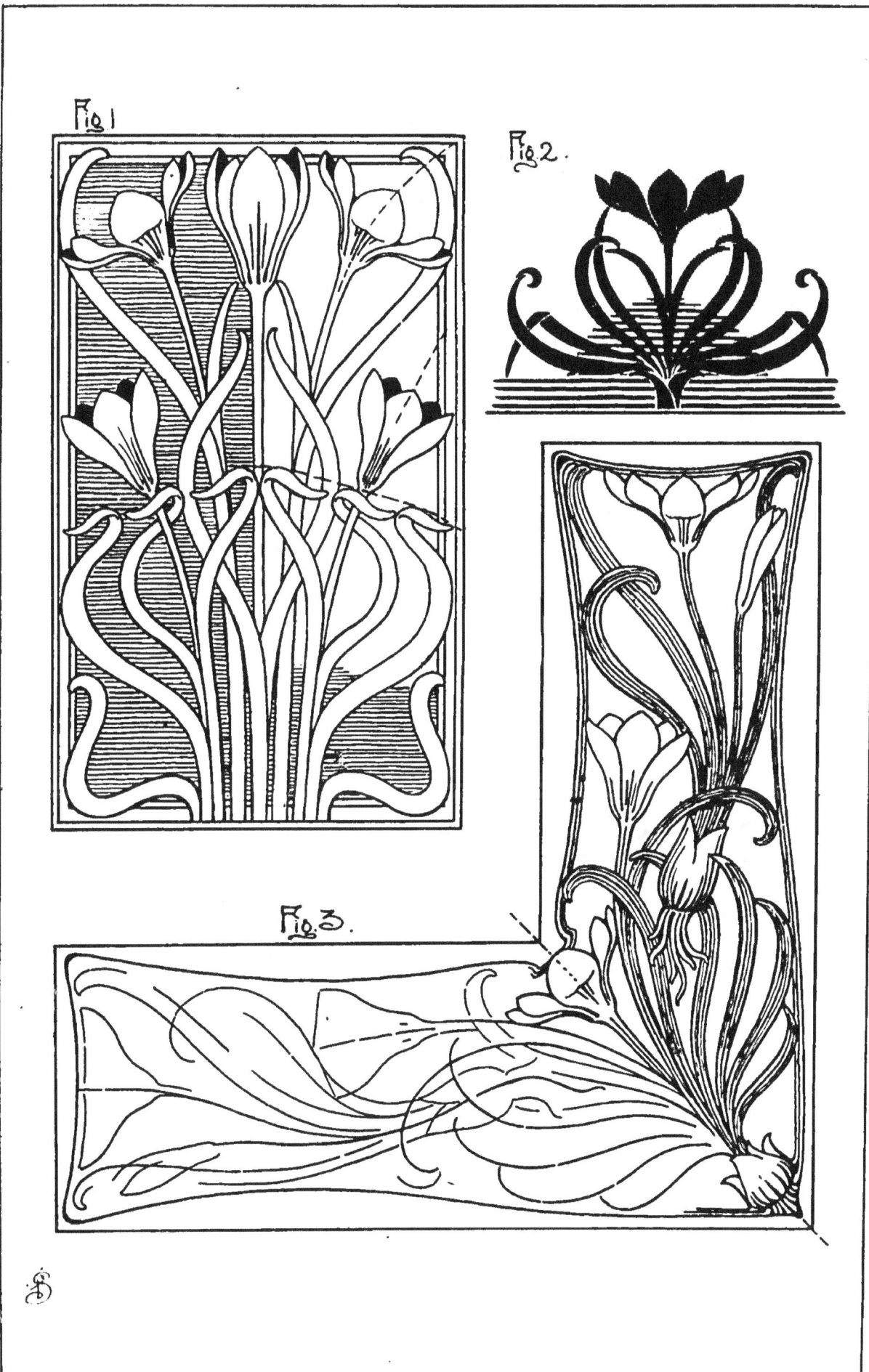

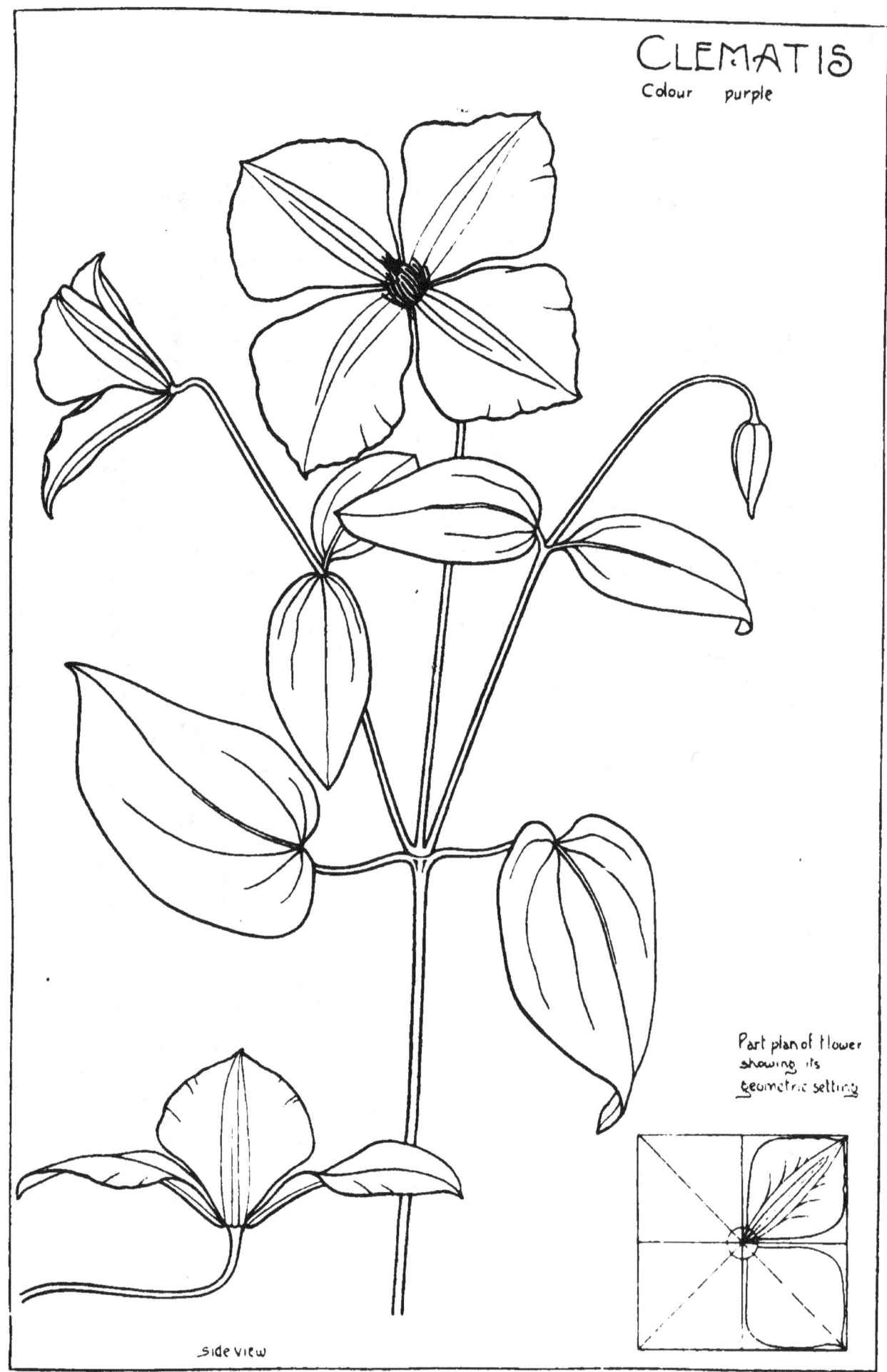

Plate XIII.

CLEMATIS
Colour purple

Part plan of flower showing its geometric setting

side view

Plate XIV.

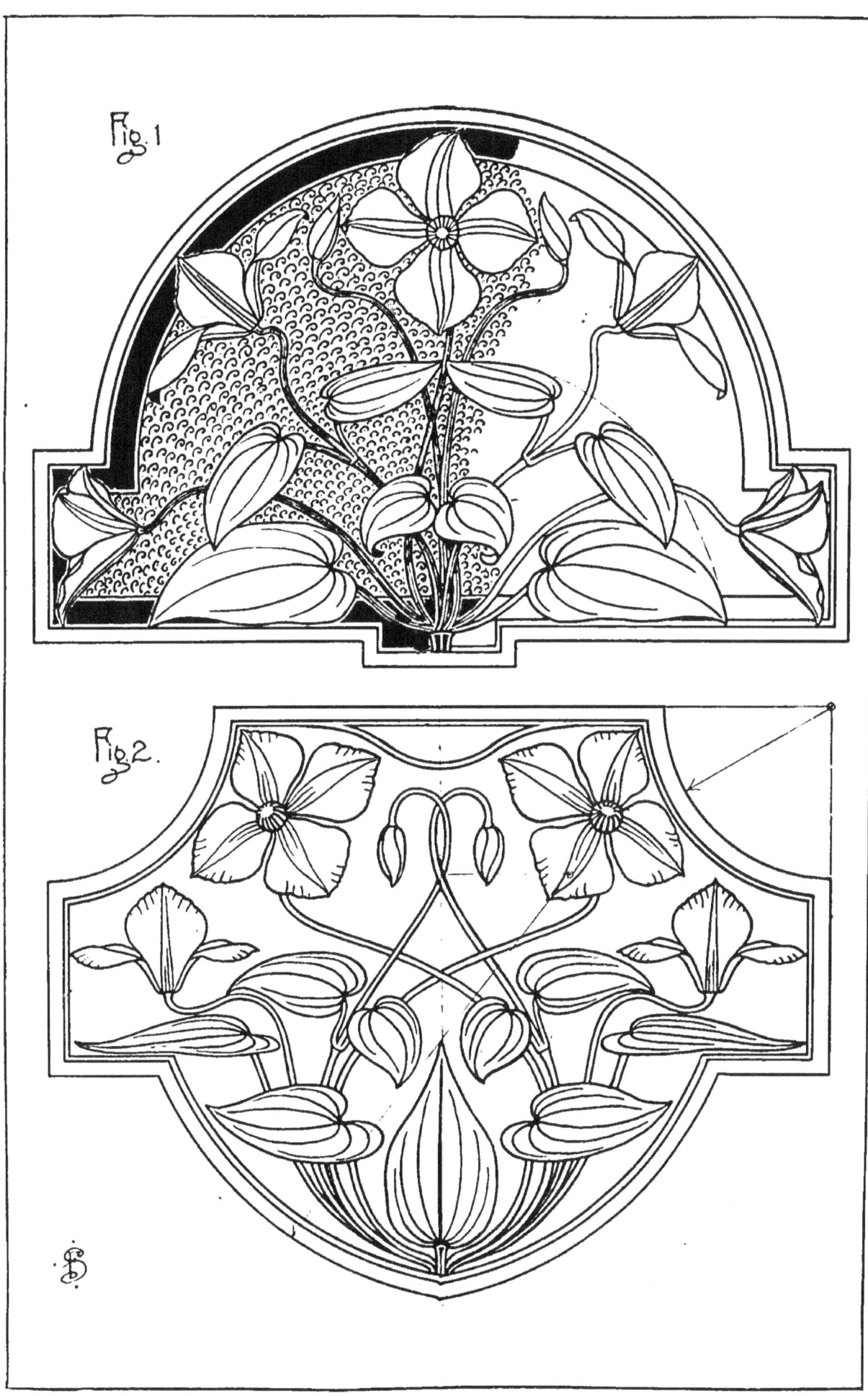

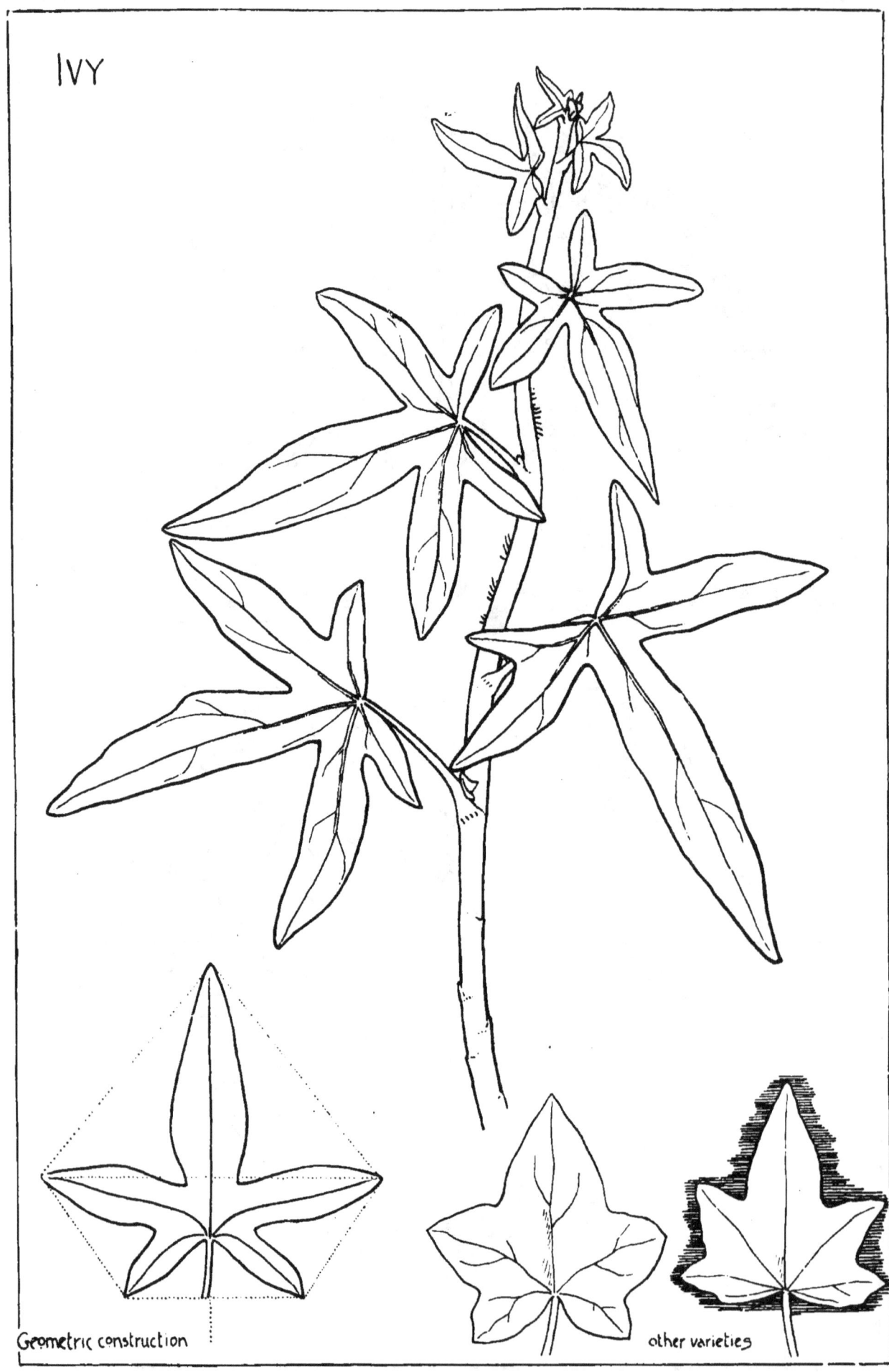

Plate XV.

IVY

Geometric construction   other varieties

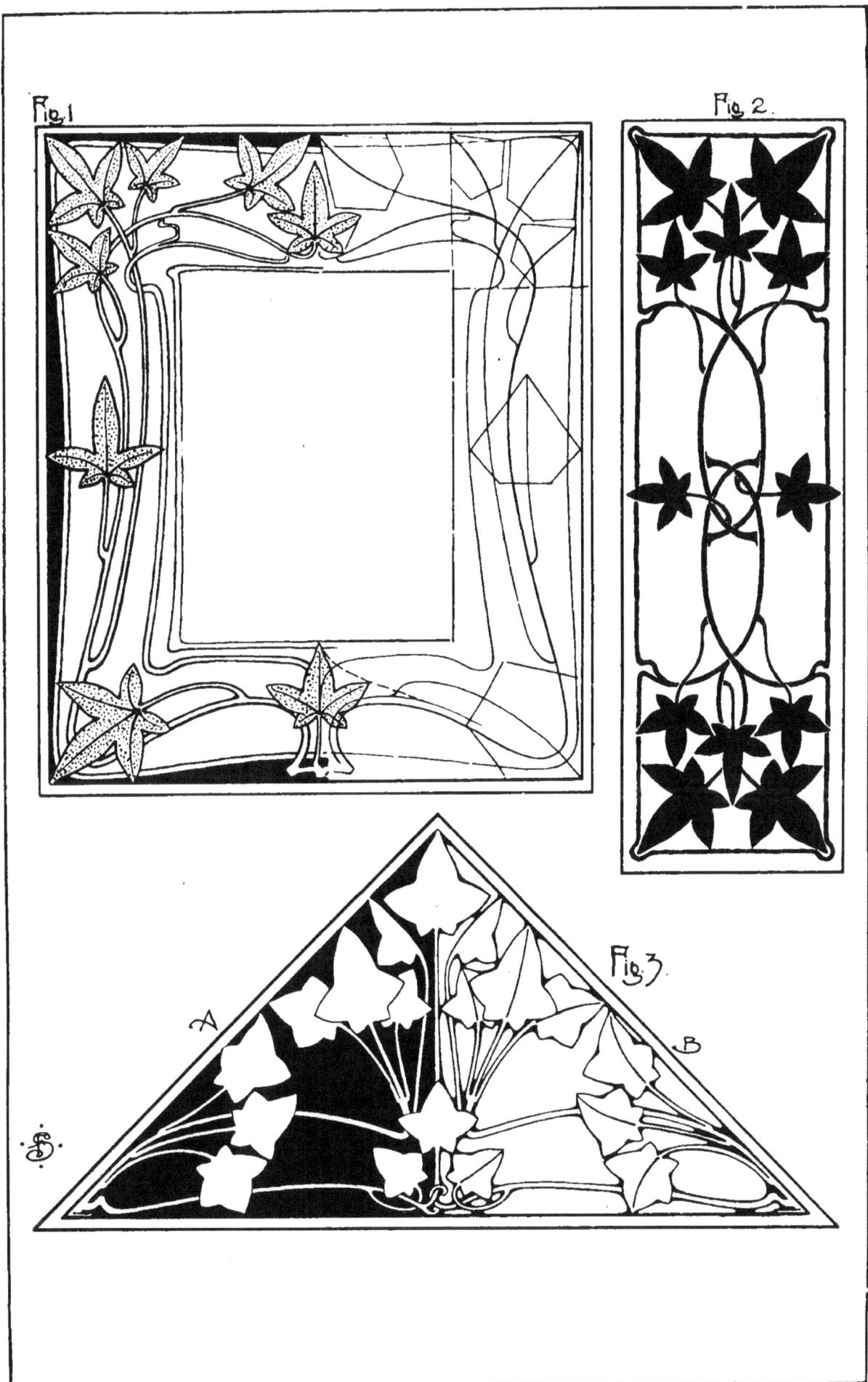

Plate XVI.

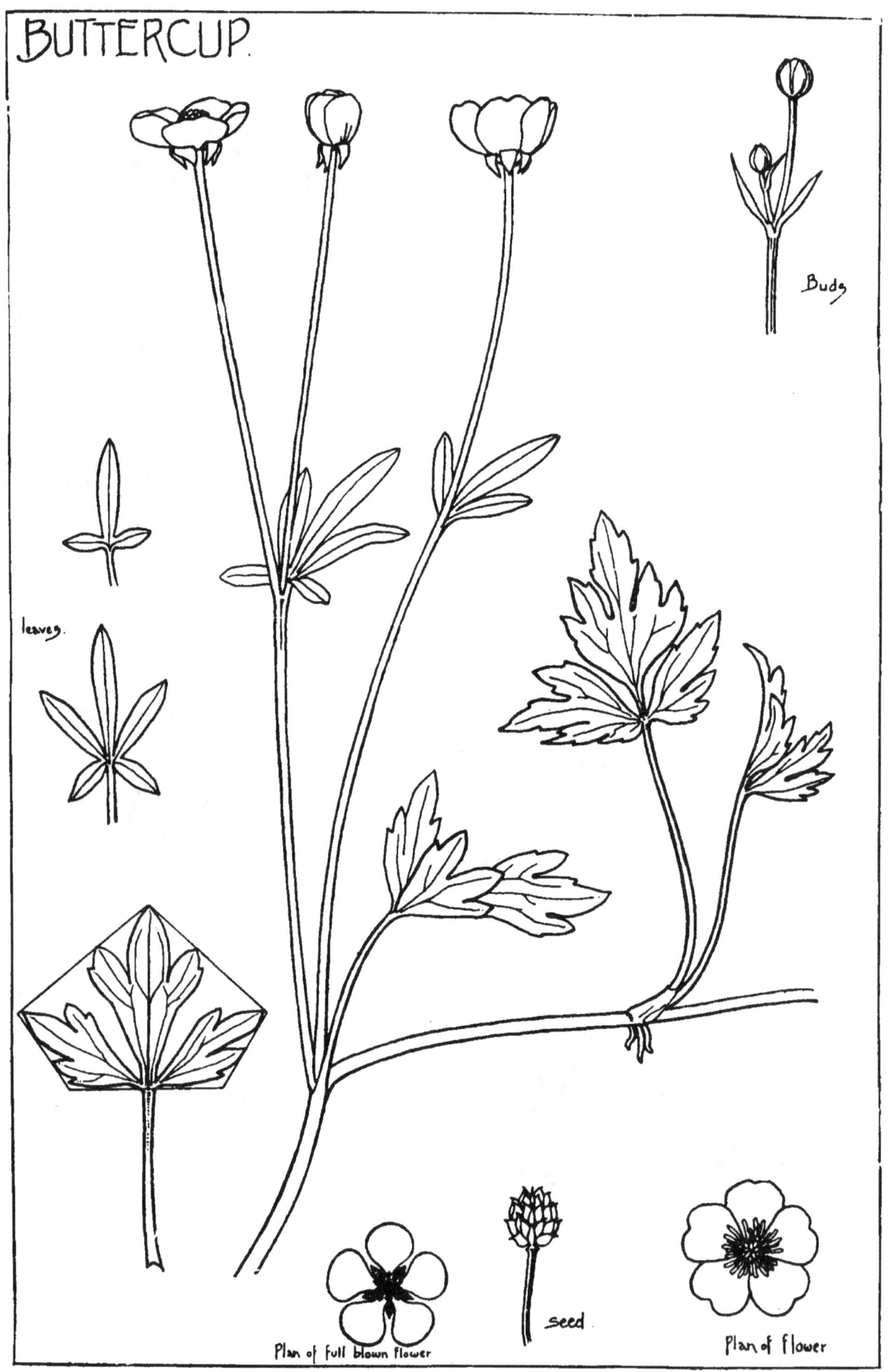

Plate XVIII.

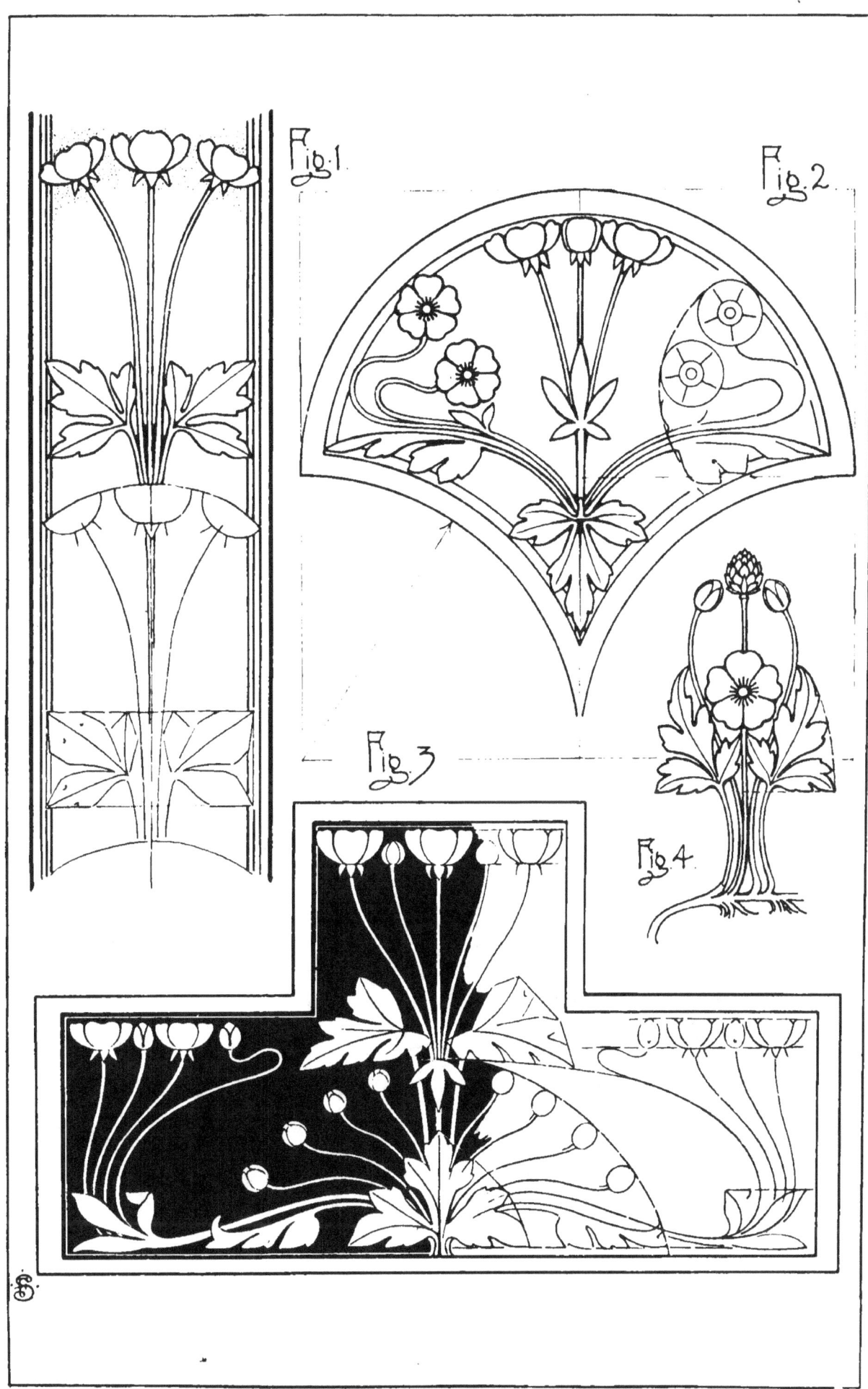

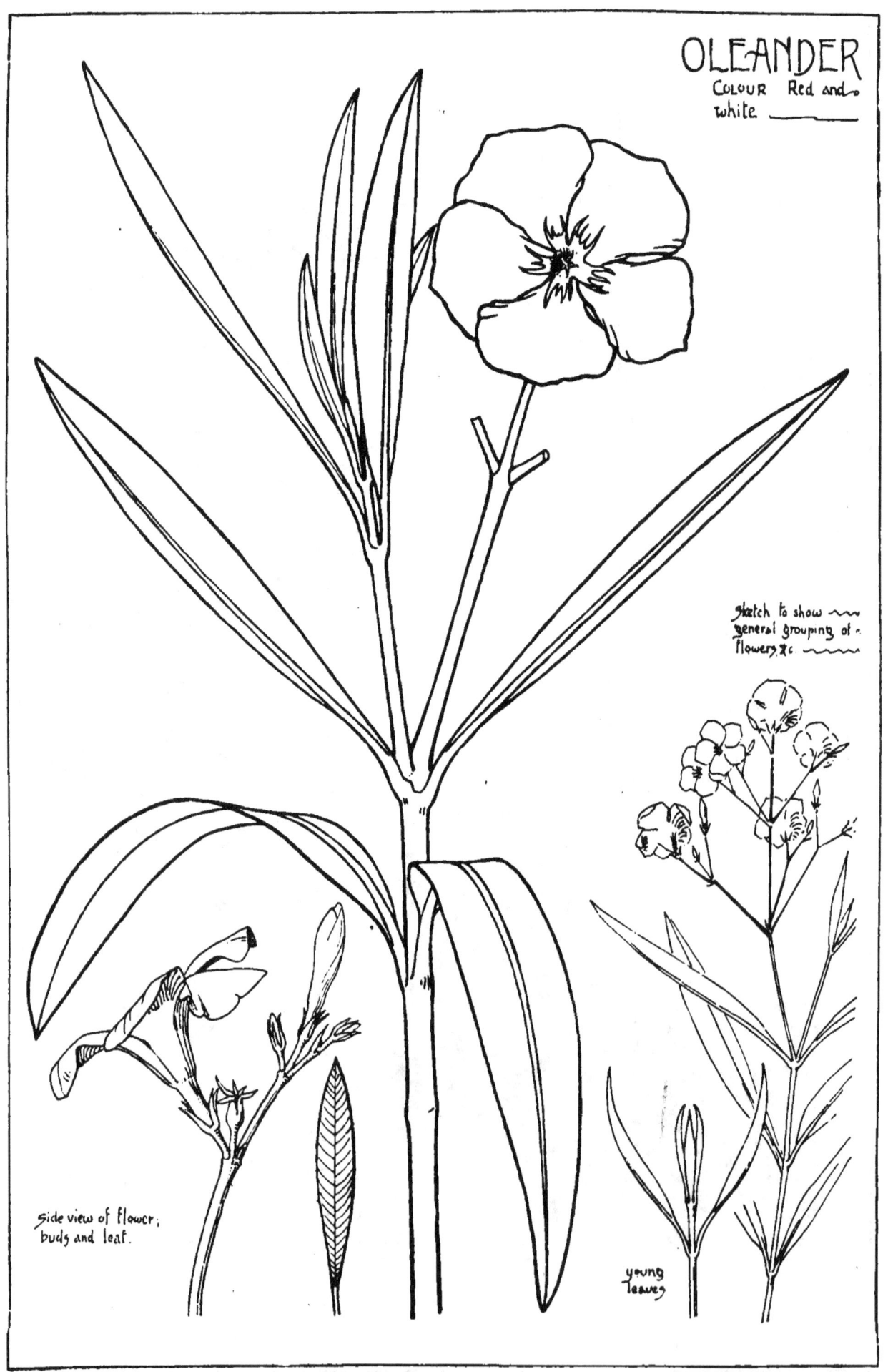

Plate XIX.

OLEANDER
Colour Red and white

Plate XX.

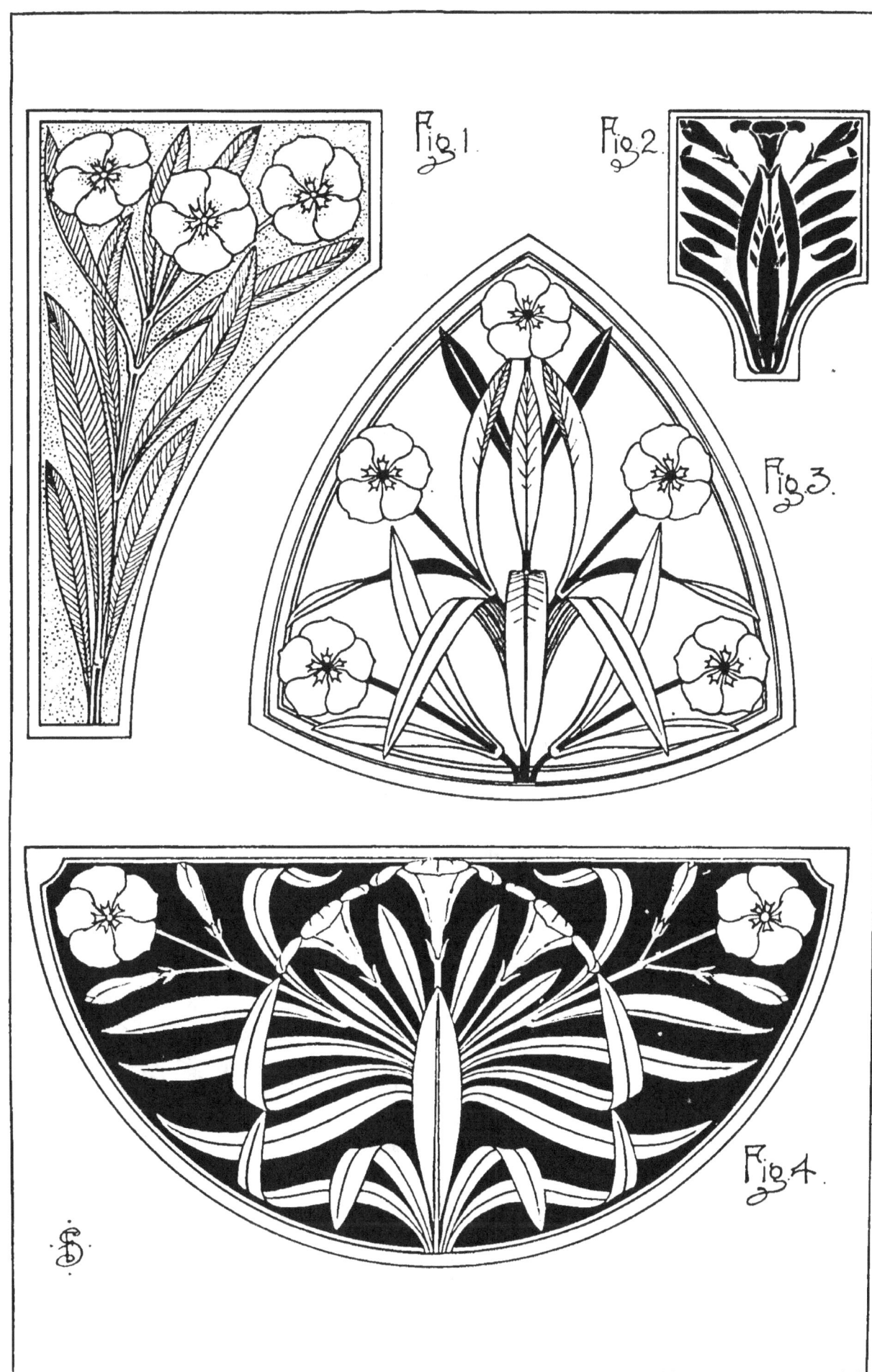

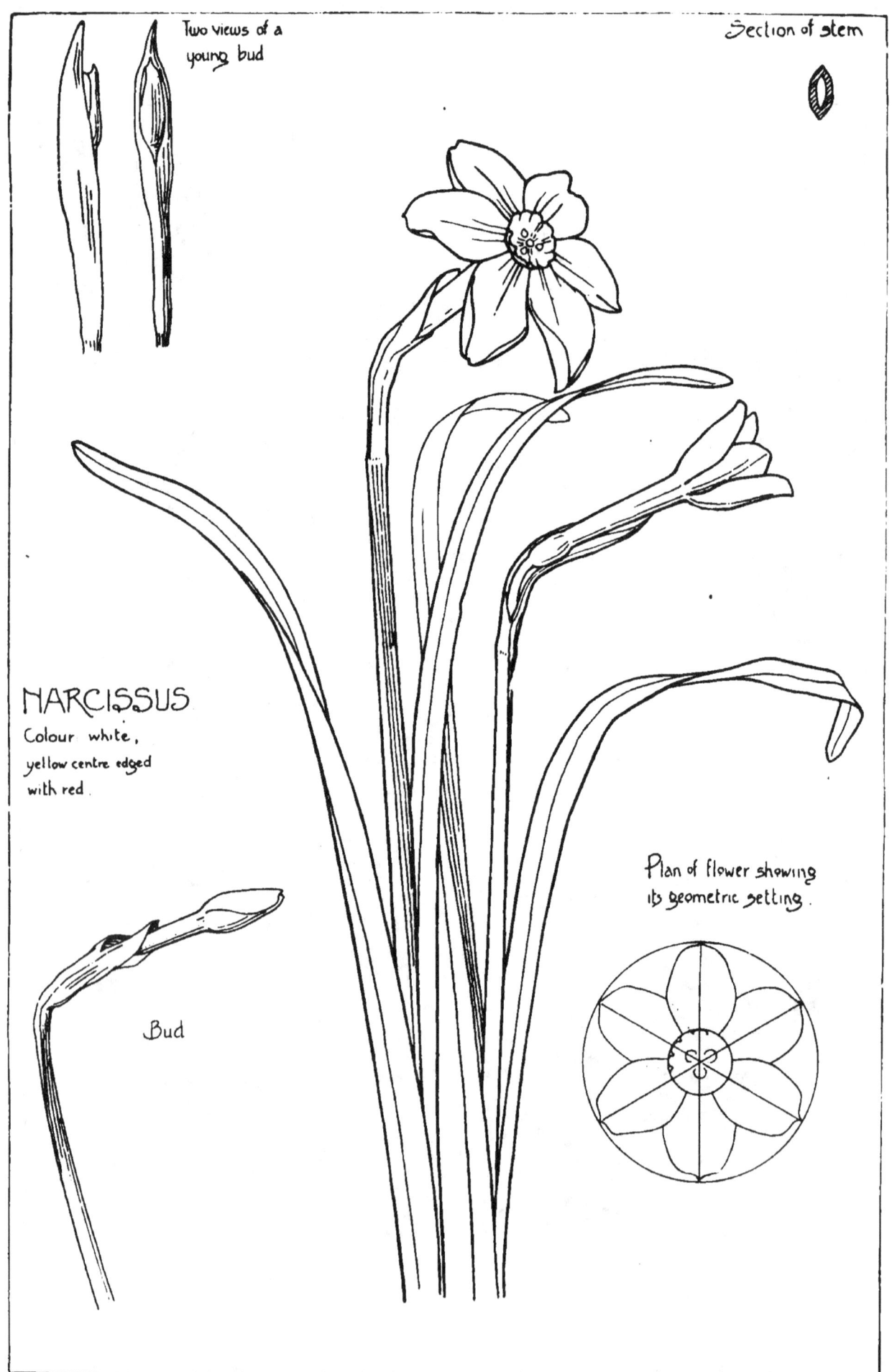

Plate XXI.

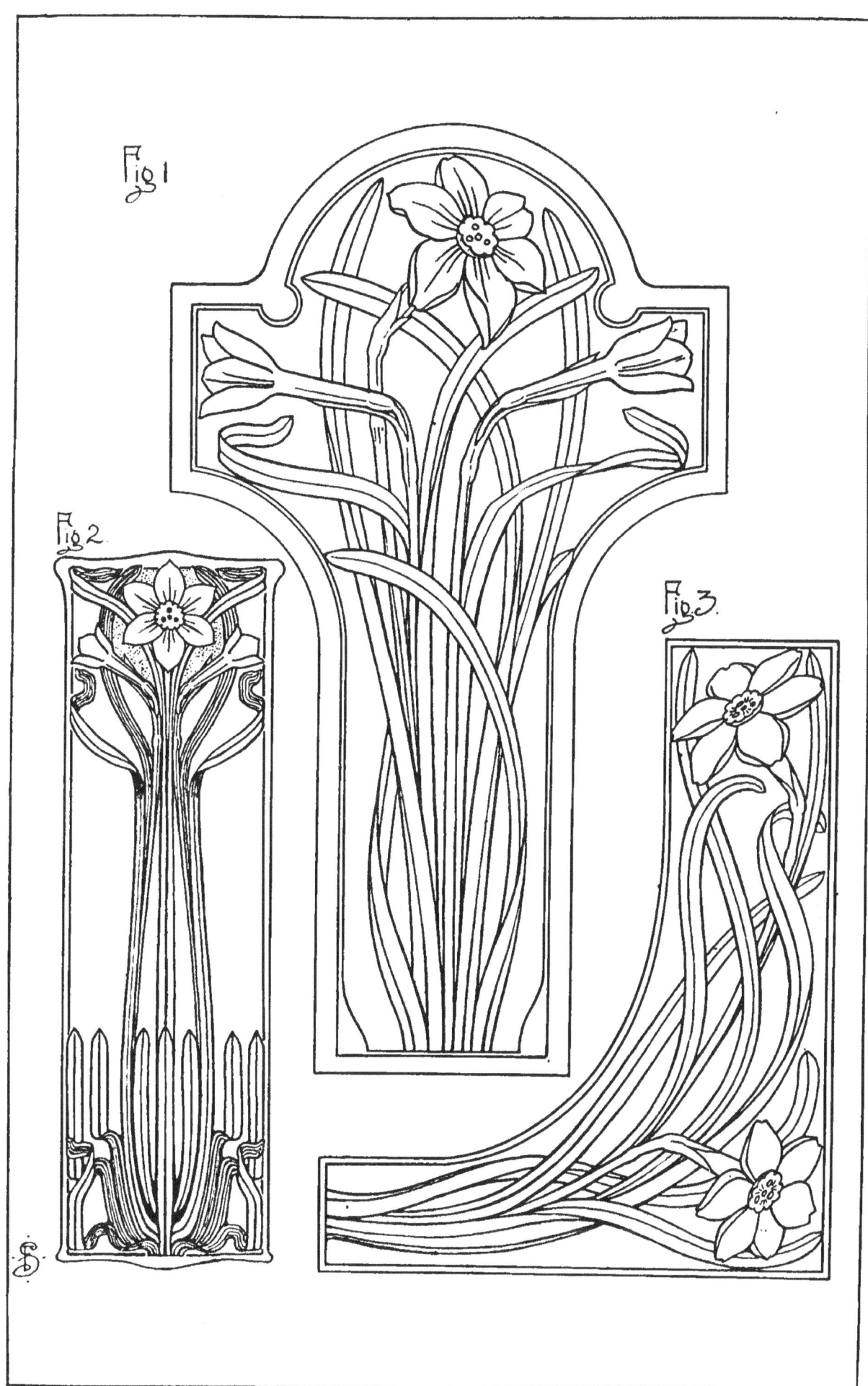

Plate XXII.

Plate XXIII.

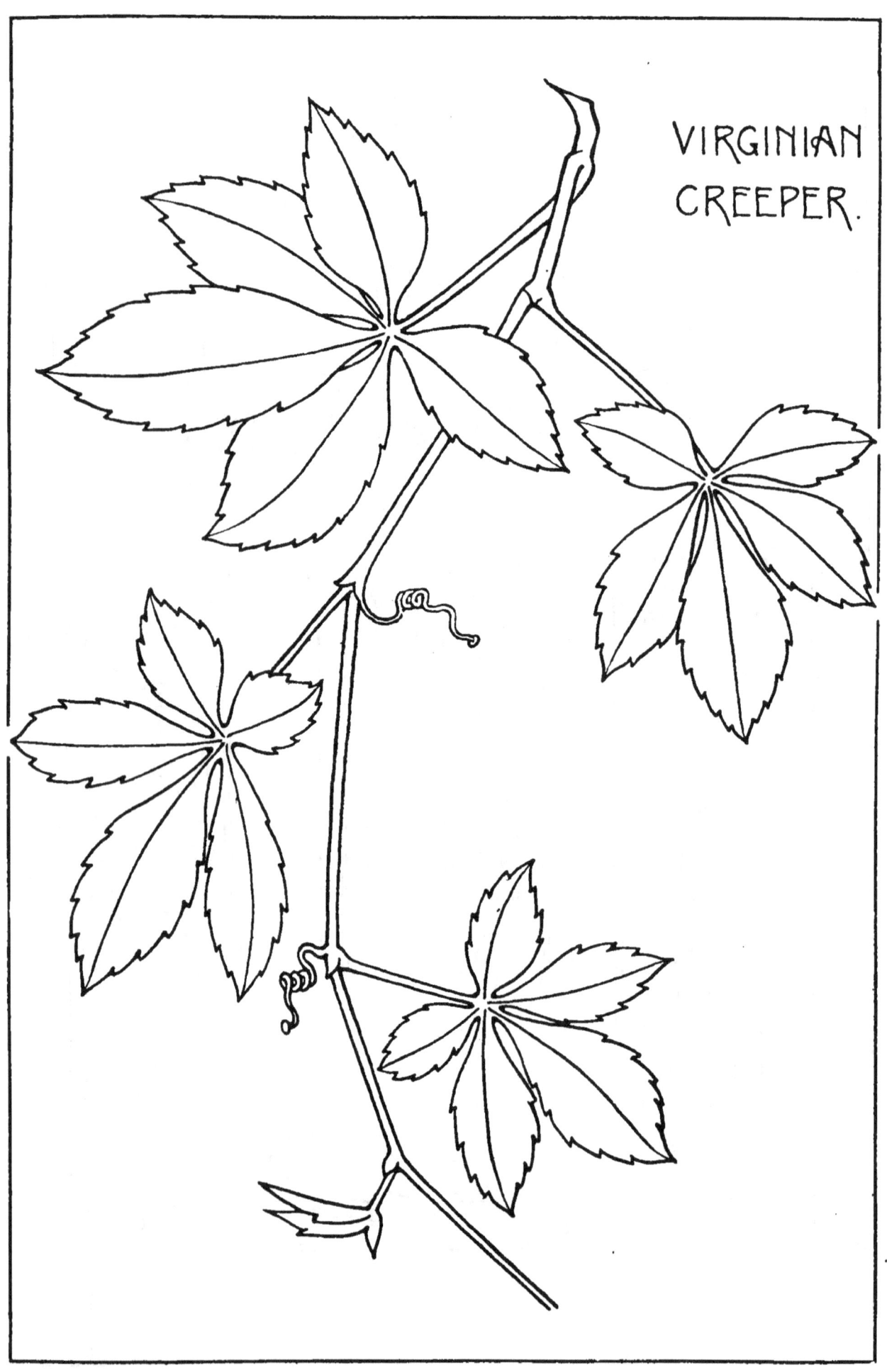

VIRGINIAN CREEPER.

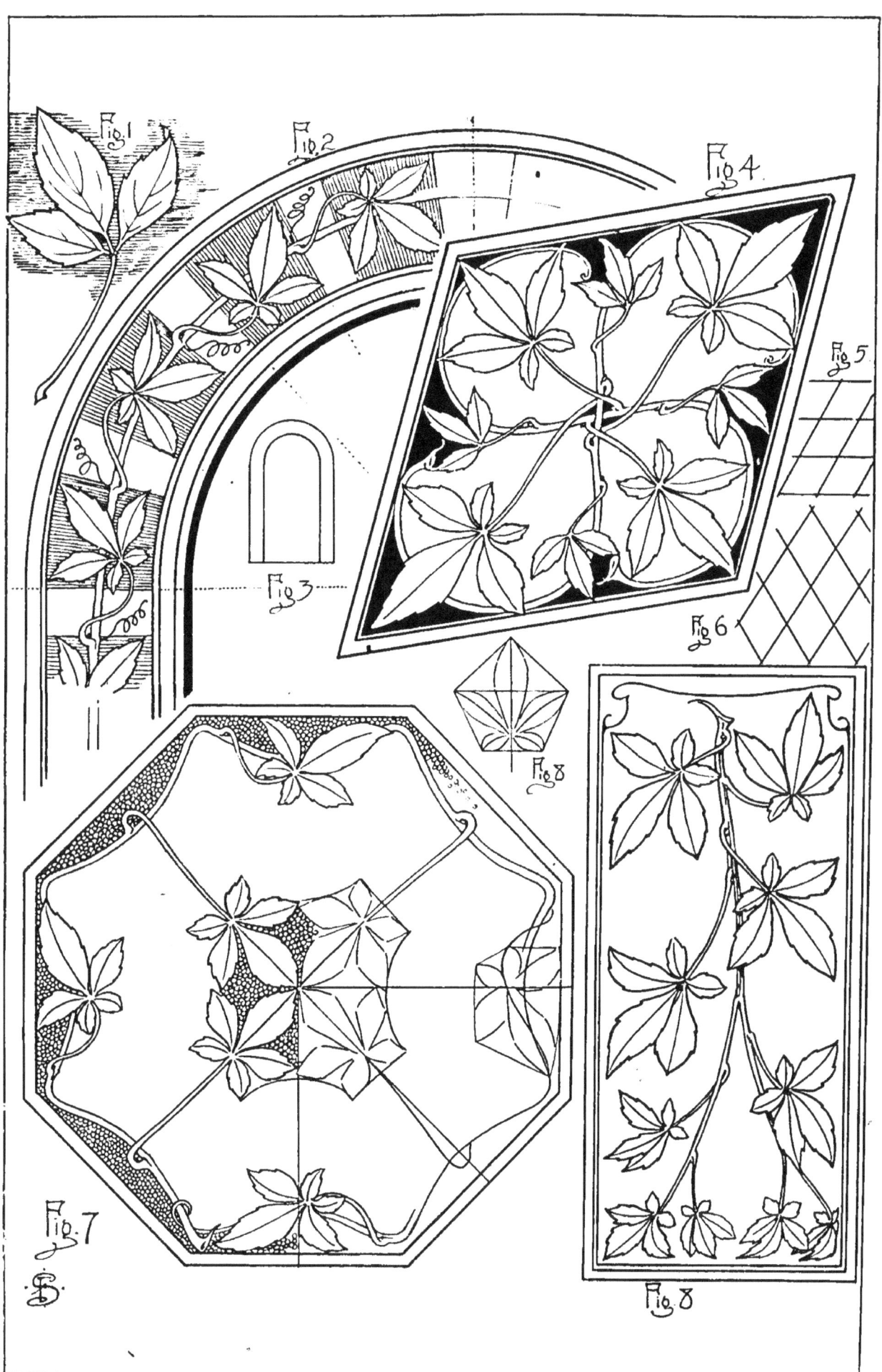

Plate XXIV.

www.ingramcontent.com/pod-product-compliance
Lightning Source LLC
Chambersburg PA
CBHW082259220526
45469CB00009B/3069